MAGIC SUTRAS POTENT

Ashwini Kumar Aggarwal

जय गुरुदेव

© 2018, Author

ISBN13: 978-93-5321-773-0 Paperback Edition
ISBN13: 978-93-95766-43-2 Hardbound Edition
ISBN13: 978-93-5321-832-4 Digital Edition

This work is licensed under a Creative Commons Attribution 4.0 International License. Please visit https://creativecommons.org/licenses/by/4.0/

Title: **Magic Sutras Potent**
Author: **Ashwini Kumar Aggarwal**

Printed and Published by
Devotees of Sri Sri Ravi Shankar Ashram
34 Sunny Enclave, Devigarh Road,
Patiala 147001, Punjab, India

https://advaita56.in/
The Art of Living Centre

https://www.artofliving.org/

27th July 2018 Friday, Guru Poornima, Vyasa Full Moon Shukla Paksha, Varsha Ritu, Aashada Masa, Dakshinayana Vikram Samvat 2075 Virodhakrit, Saka Samvat 1940 Vilambi

1st Edition July 2018

जय गुरुदेव

Preface

On a beautiful morning, as the breeze blew softly, with the hint of a coolness, the Sutras sprouted and blossomed. As the calmness filtered through and nourished them, they Magically took wing.

There was a fragrance of sandalwood that was strong and at the same time ethereal. Unknown seemed its source. It lingered for an imperceptible moment, and was gone in a flash.

There are times when one is d e e p l y Grateful.

Gratefulness is simply one of the countless points when the divine intersects one's path. Then the loving G r a c e that is abundantly showering is Fortunately **received**.

It is called पात्रता, i.e. one is eligible. The application has been successfully passed.

> 7 sutras, just seven dictums culled from PATANJALI YOGA SUTRAS solve the equation. Bring us home.

Blessing

"In Meditation, healing can happen. When the mind is calm, alert and totally contented, then it is like a laser beam – it is very powerful and healing can happen."

Life poses a million opportunities to be grateful and a billion opportunities to grumble. But having a Guru surpasses all of this - it takes you to another plane and opens your eyes to another reality - a shift in your consciousness to see, and experience the oneness with the universe. 27th July 2018, San Mateo, California (10:30am PDT, 11pm IST)

Gurudev Sri Sri Ravi Shankar

Table of Contents

Preface 3
Blessing 4
The 1st Sutra Dictum 7
The 2nd Sutra Dictum 9
The 3rd Sutra Dictum 11
The 4th Sutra Dictum 13
The 5th Sutra Dictum 15
The 6th Sutra Dictum 17
The 7th Sutra Dictum 19
Foundation Sutra 22
Nuts And Bolts 23
Sutra Dictums Summed Up 24
Patanjali Yoga Sutras With Dictums 25
Meditation 26
The Sanskrit Alphabet 27
Pronunciation Of Sanskrit Letters 27
References 28
Gratefulness 29
Epilogue 30

The 1st Sutra Dictum

Friendliness maitrī मैत्री

Friendliness is the starting point. A new born baby is so friendly. It is friendly towards one and all; towards people, animals, plants and flowers.

Friendship is a great virtue. It melts stress and strain. It dissolves bitterness and pain. It gives rise to self-confidence and self-esteem. It brings one close to nature and the subtle realms.

An aura of amicability is the stepping stone to success.

PATANJALI YOGA SUTRAS
Aphorism 1.33 from Samadhi Pada

मैत्रीकरुणामुदितोपेक्षाणां सुखदुःखपुण्यापुण्यविषयाणां

भावनातश्चित्तप्रसादनम् । १.३३

maitrīkaruṇāmuditopekṣāṇāṁ sukhaduḥkhapuṇyāpuṇyaviṣayāṇāṁ

bhāvanātaścittaprasādanam I

मैत्री-करुणा-मुदिता-उपेक्षाणां सुख-दुःख-पुण्य-अपुण्य-विषयाणां भावनातः चित्त-प्रसादनम् ।

1.33 By cultivating an attitude of Friendliness, Compassion, Delight, Disregard towards Happy, Sad, Righteous, evilMinded people respectively; peace of mind can be achieved

Peace of mind and subjugation of the Obstacles can also be achieved by cultivating an attitude of
- *maitrī = Friendliness towards the Sukhi = Successful and Happy people*
- *karuṇā = Compassion towards the Duḥkhi = Sad and Unsuccessful people*
- *muditā = Delight in the activities of the Righteous people*
- *upekṣā = Ignoring and disregarding the activities of the Unrighteous and evilminded people.*

Friendship begins at the first chakra, the mooladhara. Associated with the Earth element that is firm. Friendship is another name for Enthusiasm in life.

Friendliness ->

The 2nd Sutra Dictum

Compassion karuṇā करुणा

Compassion is so huge. It is something that envelops all. Compassion is the product of a mature mind. It is the attribute that makes one real friends with the Lord and his Lordship.

Compassion opens all doors. It bridges all gaps.

> PATANJALI YOGA SUTRAS
> Aphorism 1.33 from Samadhi Pada

मैत्रीकरुणामुदितोपेक्षाणां सुखदुःखपुण्यापुण्यविषयाणां

भावनातश्चित्तप्रसादनम् । १.३३

1.33 By cultivating an attitude of Friendliness, Compassion, Delight, Disregard towards Happy, Sad, Righteous, evilMinded people respectively; peace of mind can be achieved

Friendliness expands to become Compassion. When one's mind soars, it can identify with a much larger landscape and emotional spectrum.

That is why the scriptures say, out of compassion, the Lord assumes a human form to interact with us as a Saint, a Guru, a Master.

Compassion begins at the second chakra, the swadhisthana. Associated with the Water element that flows. Compassion is another name for Kindness in life, extending a helping hand, reaching out, sharing with the unknown.

Friendliness -> Compassion ->

The 3rd Sutra Dictum

Happiness mudita मुदिता

Happiness sprouts from Compassion. When one can merge in the nature of things, then one senses true happiness.

Compassion blossoms as the Fountain of Joy.

PATANJALI YOGA SUTRAS
Aphorism 1.33 from Samadhi Pada

मैत्रीकरुणामुदितोपेक्षाणां सुखदुःखपुण्यापुण्यविषयाणां

भावनातश्चित्तप्रसादनम् । १.३३

1.33 By cultivating an attitude of Friendliness, Compassion, Delight, Disregard towards **Happy, Sad, Righteous, evilMinded people respectively; peace of mind can be achieved**

Delighting in this creation. Being happy with oneself. Enjoying with someone or something. It is a fine tribute to a human birth.

Happiness begins at the third chakra, the manipura. Associated with the Fire element that crackles in exuberant joy. Joy is another name for success in life; joy is infectious and spreads all around.

Friendliness -> Compassion -> Happiness ->

The 4th Sutra Dictum

Fearlessness kūrma_nādī कूर्मनाडी

When joy has welled up, Peace dawns. Fearlessness becomes rooted. And one can sense the loosening of shackles. Happiness results in the Peace of Fearlessness.

> PATANJALI YOGA SUTRAS
> Aphorism 3.31 from Vibhooti Pada

कूर्मनाड्यां स्थैर्यम् ॥ ३.३१ ॥ kūrmanādyāṁ sthairyam ॥3.31
कूर्म-नाडयां स्थैर्यम् ॥

3.31 On the **kūrma_nādī** develops Steadfastness

Sanyam on the Kurma Nadi develops freedom from fears of ups-and-downs. Mind becomes firm. Fickleness vanishes. Fears give rise to innumerable, far-reaching unwarranted actions and words, so this technique of soothing misgivings assumes great importance. Traditionally a tortoise is the symbol of stability. kūrma_nādī = Trachea = tortoise tube = food pipe = area of chest where hand goes to stabilize oneself or to show sign of fear or discomfort.

Steadfastness simply means stable breath. Normal breathing is the sign of peace. It is the quality of fearlessness. Lightness arises from joy. Calmness is the product of steady breathing.

Fearlessness begins at the fourth chakra, the anahata. Associated with the Air element that moves unpredictably and becomes still as well. Fearlessness is another name for Steadfastness, which also means that the heartbeat is sound and stable. It is the precursor to great achievements in life.

Friendliness -> Compassion -> Happiness -> Fearlessness

The 5th Sutra Dictum

Freedom   kaṇṭha_kūpa   कण्ठकूप

Fearlessness gives rise to Freedom. One can sense a continuous source of prana within. That in turn begins to wipe out the Sanskaras.

Freedom results in erasing of the Impressions. The tendencies and notions melt away. Obsession and Rigidity goes away. A lasting Bliss has taken birth.

> PATANJALI YOGA SUTRAS
> Aphorism 3.30 from Vibhooti Pada

कण्ठकूपे क्षुत्पिपासानिवृत्तिः ॥ ३.३० ॥

kaṇṭhakūpe kṣutpipāsānivṛttiḥ ॥3.30

कण्ठ-कूपे क्षुत्-पिपासा-निवृत्तिः ॥

3.30 On the **kaṇṭha_kūp** fosters cessation of hunger and thirst

Sanyam on the Well of the Throat helps ease pangs of hunger and thirst by stimulating the Vagus nerve. We can go without eating and drinking. Also if the occasion demands, we can eat properly and enjoy all dishes.

kaṇṭha_kūpa = *Deep Throat, WellofThroat, Throat cavity, Throat pit*
kṣut = *hunger*, pipāsā = *thirst*, nivṛttiḥ = *cessation*

A very important technique, since hunger and thirst are primal needs and these desires in turn lead to bigger ones like lust, obsession and frantic-shopping. This Sanyam curbs those as well.

(And what are hunger and thirst? Latent impressions. Sanskaras that drive us to covet, crave and hanker for.)

Freedom begins at the fifth chakra, the vishuddhi. Associated with the Space element that is all pervading. Freedom is another name for disassociation with pain. Disassociation from limiting habits, patterns, and opinions. Freedom also means that none is inimical, so there is no impression or karma.

Friendliness -> Compassion -> Happiness -> Fearlessness -> Freedom ->

The 6th Sutra Dictum

Glow of Purity jyotiṣ_matī ज्योतिष्मती

Purity shines forth from one's being. The aura reflects the glories of creation. The saintliness is there for all to see. Freedom results in Purity. Bright Intellect. Brilliant Personality. As the mind becomes effulgent, only brilliant thoughts erupt. All modulations become bright as the Divine. Freedom makes one Shine. Our outer being glows and our status in society rises high.

> **PATANJALI YOGA SUTRAS**
> Aphorism 1.36 from Samadhi Pada

विशोका वा ज्योतिष्मती ॥ १.३६ ॥ viśokā vā jyotiṣmatī ॥ 1.36
विशोका वा ज्योतिष्मती ।

1.36 Or the Luminous_Intellect Vanquishes Sorrow

Or in the company of the one having a Brilliant Intellect, sadness is gone. Sorrow vanquishes in the presence of an enlightened Master. We can overcome sorrow by contemplating on the Brilliant. The wise have this effect of brushing off on us, just as gold makes anything reflect and shine. That is the quality of a Guru.

Effulgence begins at the sixth chakra, the ajna. When one radiates the wisdom, the saintliness, the decency, the gentlemanliness. One reaches the state that is beyond the purview of the five elements, or no longer limited by the considerations of space-time. A state unaffected by the laws of creation.

Friendliness -> Compassion -> Happiness -> Fearlessness -> Freedom -> Glow of Purity ->

The 7th Sutra Dictum

Witness Consciousness divya _dṛṣṭi दिव्यदृष्टि

Finally one's vision becomes totally pure. One's attitude, opinion and point-of-view simply mirror the divinity. Divine Vision.

And then there is nothing to do. One has dropped all efforts. One rests, having become a Witness. The trials and tribulations have all disappeared. The struggles have surrendered themselves. One's will has merged in the Divine.

PATANJALI YOGA SUTRAS
Aphorism 1.3 from Samadhi Pada

तदा द्रष्टुः स्वरूपेऽवस्थानम् ॥ १.३ ॥

tadā draṣṭuḥ svarūpe'vasthānam ॥ 1.3 ॥

तदा द्रष्टुः स्वरूपे अवस्थानम् ।

1.3 Then one realizes the Seer's essential Nature

Divine Vision is manifest at the seventh chakra, the sahasrara. This is un-observable by the senses. It is not cognizable by the intellect. It is a state of innocence and simplicity that defies all logic. A state of bliss that sustains, that is unstained. Another name for purity.

By living a yogic life, we are able to get a glimpse of the ultimate reality. We are able to become one with the laws of the Universe, nay transcend all.

This presuppose that one has been observing one's responsibilities and duties and following one's practices in daily life, as stated by

> Aphorism 2.29 from the Sadhana Pada

यमनियमासनप्राणायामप्रत्याहारधारणाध्यानसमाधयोऽष्टावङ्गानि

॥ २.२९ ॥

yamaniyamāsanaprāṇāyāmapratyāhāradhāraṇādhyānasamādhayo'ṣṭāvaṅgāni ॥ 2.29 ॥

यम-नियम-आसन-प्राणायाम-प्रत्याहार-धारणा-ध्यान-समाधयः अष्टौ-अङ्गानि ।

2.29 Eight Limbs are Yama, Niyama, Asana, Pranayama, Partyahara, Dharana, Dhyana and Samadhi

These are the limbs of Yoga, the Divine path. Limbs because each helps the other, being steady in anyone will strengthen the others also.

> Patanjali sums up –
> Aphorism 4.34 from Kaivalya Pada

पुरुषार्थशून्यानां गुणानां प्रतिप्रसवः कैवल्यं स्वरूपप्रतिष्ठा वा चितिशक्तिरिति ॥ ४.३४ ॥

puruṣārthaśūnyānāṁ guṇānāṁ pratiprasavaḥ kaivalyaṁ svarūpapratiṣṭhā vā citiśaktiriti ॥ 4.34 ॥

पुरुषार्थ-शून्यानां गुणानां प्रतिप्रसवः कैवल्यं स्वरूप-प्रतिष्ठा वा चिति-शक्तिः इति ॥

4.34 Kaivalyam is being established in the Center, when no more Aims exist, when Gunas are reabsorbed; or the Power of Consciousness

Liberation as Living in the Center,
where no aims exist, when the Gunas are reabsorbed.

Friendliness -> Compassion -> Happiness -> Fearlessness -> Freedom -> Glow of Purity -> Witness Consciousness.

Foundation Sutra

Patanjali gives a rare insight in

Aphorism 2.27 from the Sadhana Pada

तस्य सप्तधा प्रान्तभूमिः प्रज्ञा ॥२.२७॥

tasya saptadhā prāntabhūmiḥ prajñā ‖ 2.27 ‖

तस्य सप्तधा प्रान्त-भूमिः प्रज्ञा ।
2.27 Awareness comprises of a Seven-Tier-Rise to the Final-State.

The final state of Awareness attained by the Yogi or the Enlightened comprises of seven sequential steps.

Nuts and Bolts

Our Rishis were top scientists who had made a remarkable discovery. They had fathomed that the space was the starting point. Mind space, a subtler entity than the gross space.

From the thoughts in the mind, one's whole creation got formed. Our impressions, drives and impulses became the foundations of our existence.

The events and situations and peoples around us were largely the result of our own temperament and attitude. So it was essential to nurture and groom the thoughts. Thus they gave us the Sutras. And it was left to the Saints across time, culture and region to make the Sutras work for their devotees.

Inducing good intentions within produces corresponding waves outside. This fact even though simple to state is quite hard to put into practice regularly. It is the Guru who makes it doable.

Sutra Dictums summed up

1. **Friendliness** maitrī मैत्री

2. **Compassion** karuṇā करुणा

3. **Happiness** muditā मुदिता

4. **Fearlessness** kūrma_nādī कूर्मनाडी

5. **Freedom** kaṇṭha_kūpa कण्ठकूप

6. **Glow of Purity** jyotiṣ_matī ज्योतिष्मती

7. **Witness Consciousness** divya_dṛṣṭi दिव्यदृष्टि

Patanjali Yoga Sutras with Dictums

मैत्रीकरुणामुदितोपेक्षाणां सुखदुःखपुण्यापुण्यविषयाणां
भावनातश्चित्तप्रसादनम् । १.३३
maitrīkaruṇāmuditopekṣāṇāṁ
sukhaduḥkhapuṇyāpuṇyaviṣayāṇāṁ
bhāvanātaścittaprasādanam || 1.33 ||

कूर्मनाड्यां स्थैर्यम् ॥३.३१॥
kūrmanāḍyāṁ sthairyam || 3.31 ||

कण्ठकूपे क्षुत्पिपासानिवृत्तिः ॥३.३०॥
kaṇṭhakūpe kṣutpipāsānivṛttiḥ || 3.30 ||

विशोका वा ज्योतिष्मती ॥१.३६॥
viśokā vā jyotiṣmatī || 1.36 ||

तदा द्रष्टुः स्वरूपेऽवस्थानम् ॥१.३॥
tadā draṣṭuḥ svarūpe'vasthānam || 1.3 ||

यमनियमासनप्राणायामप्रत्याहारधारणाध्यानसमाधयोऽष्टावङ्गानि ॥ २.२९
yamaniyamāsanaprāṇāyāmapratyāhāradhāraṇādhyānas
amādhayo'ṣṭāvaṅgāni || 2.29 ||

पुरुषार्थशून्यानां गुणानां प्रतिप्रसवः कैवल्यं स्वरूपप्रतिष्ठा वा चितिशक्तिरिति
॥४.३४॥
puruṣārthaśūnyānāṁ guṇānāṁ pratiprasavaḥ kaivalyaṁ
svarūpapratiṣṭhā vā citiśaktiriti || 4.34 ||

Meditation

Meditation is sitting with the Sutras. Recalling them. Going over them one by one.

Contemplating the dictums clearly.

That makes the mind supple and soon one reaches the goal.

> Remember that the company of an enlightened master, a Guru makes it all simple.
>
> https://www.artofliving.org/
>
> https://programs.org.in/

Some preparations will be helpful to our practice. A fresh bath, a clean room with a pleasant ambience. Comfortable clothing. A proper asana or chair or sofa.

Choose a time when there are minimum interruptions and less nearby sounds. Switching off the mobile completely will be a great advantage.

The Sanskrit Alphabet

ॐ अ आ इ ई उ ऊ ऋ ॠ ऌ ॡ   ए ऐ ओ औ   अं अः

क्	ख्	ग्	घ्	ङ्	The Shiva Sounds
च्	छ्	ज्	झ्	ञ्	
ट्	ठ्	ड्	ढ्	ण्	The Brahma Sounds
त्	थ्	द्	ध्	न्	
प्	फ्	ब्	भ्	म्	The Vishnu Sounds
य् र् ल् व्		श् ष् स्		ह्	
अँ	व्ळ्		व्ह्		Vedic Sanskrit

Pronunciation of Sanskrit Letters

अ son आ father इ it ई beat उ full ऊ pool

ऋ rhythm ॠ marine ऌ revelry ॡ ए play ऐ aisle

ओ go औ loud

अँ Anusvara is pure nasal – close the lips – similar to म्

अः Visarga is Breath release like ह् and preceding vowel sound e.g. Pronounce नमः as नमह , शान्तिः as शान्तिहि , विष्णुः as विष्णुहु

क seeK	ख KHan	ग Get	घ loGHut	ङ siNG
च CHunk	छ catchhim	ज Jump	झ heDGEhog	ञ buNch
ट True	ठ anTHill	ड Drum	ढ goDHead	ण uNder
त Tamil	थ THunder	द THat	ध breaTHE	न Nut
प Put	फ Fruit	ब Bin	भ aBHor	म Much

य loYal र Red ल Luck व Vase

श Sure ष Shun स So Hum ह

References

Author	Title Edition		Year	Publisher
Sri Sri Ravi Shankar	Patanjali Yoga Sutras	1st	2010	Sri Sri Publications Trust, Bangalore
Tookaram Tatya	The Yoga Philosophy	2nd	1885	The Theosophical Society, Bombay
Swami Vivekananda	Raja Yoga: Conquering the Internal Nature	1st	1998	Advaita Ashrama Kolkata
Surinder Shanker Anand	पातञ्जल योग (अष्टाङ्गयोग)	1st	2006	Surinder Shanker Anand, Chandigarh
Sri Swami Satchidananda	The Yoga Sutras of Patanjali (Revised)	1st	2012	Integral Yoga Publications, Buckingham, Virginia
Charles Johnston	The Yoga Sutras of Patanjali			http://www.gutenberg.org/ebooks/2526
Ashwini Kumar Aggarwal	Patanjali Yoga Sutras Essence	1st	2018	Devotees of Sri Sri Ravi Shankar Ashram, Punjab

Transliteration

https://www.ashtangayoga.info/sanskrit/transliteration/transliteration-tool/#devanagari/iso15919/

Gratefulness

There are splendid reasons to be Thankful. Each day I wake up fit and devoted.

The air is clean, so sparkling is the water.

My family is caring and so calm is the neighbourhood. Friends are just a call away.

Birds chirp happily, trees sway majestically. Sunshine filters through. The ashram is serene, docile are the cows. There is trust and faith, humility and surrender abound.

Shivaratri, Navaratri, Guru Poornima and Janmashtami are heavenly. Tera May makes up for everything. Satsangs and Guru Poojas ahoy.

Technology has given many useful gadgets. Sober scientific temperaments. Courses and Festivities keep the system pure. The Advanced Meditation Program is much sought for. SANYAM is ultimate.

Epilogue

```
Space and Time are plentiful.
Nature is benign. All of this is Guru
Grace or due to His presence.
```

सर्वे भवन्तु सुखिनः । सर्वे सन्तु निरामयाः ।

सर्वे भद्राणि पश्यन्तु । मा कश्चिद् दुःख भाग् भवेत् ॥

ॐ शान्तिः शान्तिः शान्तिः ॥

When faith has blossomed in life, Every step is led by the Divine.

Sri Sri Ravi Shankar

Om Namah Shivaya

जय गुरुदेव